Presented to:

Bev

From:

Janette

Date:

8-22-20

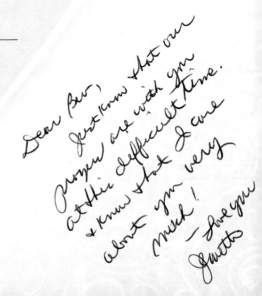

Dear Bev,
Just know that our
prayers are with you
at this difficult time.
I know that I care
about you very
much!
~ love you
Janette

*The care and support from a friend
can make all the difference when
hard times come.*

PAUL MEDLEY

until you're ready
to face the world again.

You *are* going to make it.

You *are* going to come out on top.

And I'm here to cheer you on!

The joy you're going to feel

kisses

of

Comfort

Heartwarming Messages That
Bring Assurance & Encouragement

HOWARD BOOKS
A DIVISION OF SIMON & SCHUSTER
New York   London   Toronto   Sydney

Our purpose at Howard Books is to:
- *Increase faith* in the hearts of growing Christians
- *Inspire holiness* in the lives of believers
- *Instill hope* in the hearts of struggling people everywhere
  Because He's coming again!

Published by Howard Books, a division of Simon & Schuster, Inc.
1230 Avenue of the Americas, New York, NY 10020
www.howardpublishing.com

HOWARD®

Kisses of Comfort © 2008 by Dave Bordon & Associates, LLC

ISBN-13: 978-1-4165-5864-4
ISBN-10:   1-4165-5864-0

10 9 8 7 6 5 4 3 2 1

HOWARD and colophon are registered trademarks of Simon & Schuster, Inc.

Manufactured in the United States of America

For information regarding special discounts for bulk purchases, please contact: Simon & Schuster Special Sales at 1-800-456-6798 or business@simonandschuster.com.

Project developed by Bordon Books, Tulsa, Oklahoma
Project writing and compilation by Christy Phillippe and Rayné Bordon in association with Bordon Books
Edited by Chrys Howard
Cover design by Greg Jackson, Thinkpen Design
Photo page 19 © Ron Chapple Stock/Corbis

Scripture quotations marked NLT are taken from the *Holy Bible*, New Living Translation, copyright © 1996. Used by permission of Tyndale House Publishers, Inc., Wheaton, Illinois 60189. All rights reserved.

INTRODUCTION

A kiss. It's short. Sweet. And from the heart. That's what *Kisses of Comfort* is all about. Each page of this book is a message of hope from my heart to yours, a reminder of how much I care. As you read, I hope you'll remember that no matter what happens, in sunshine or rain, I'll always be here for you.

May our Lord Jesus Christ himself and God our Father, . . . comfort you and strengthen you.

2 THESSALONIANS 2:16–17 NLT

1

You, my dear one,
have been on my heart.

I've been praying for you
that God would strengthen you
and give you hope.

I know that you are facing
a difficult challenge

and wondering if your life will ever be happy again.

But please know
that I am here for you—
to hug you tight,

to be a listening ear,

*t*o hold your hand,

and to pray that God will
shower you with His love.

You are not alone!

You have the strength you need to
make it through this

because your heavenly Father

is with you . . .

and your friends are too.

My prayer for you is this:

When you wake up in the morning,
may you have the courage
to face the day,

and when you lie down
at night, may your sleep be
restful and sweet,

because the Mighty One is
looking after you, and He is bigger
than any challenge you face.

He is the One who hung the stars

and fashioned

delicate flowers.

He is the One who crafted
the mountains,

and even the wind and sea
obey Him.

And He wants to use His great
power to help you in your time
of need.

So call upon Him today—pour out
your heart before Him.

He in turn will send you
a bouquet of His love,

and you will praise Him.

He will put a spring in your step,

and a song in your heart,

He will turn your mourning
into dancing,

and your desert will bloom.

The dryness in your life will be
returned to living waters

because God has promised
to never abandon you,

and He always keeps His promises.

He has mapped out a special
plan for your life,

and He is weaving
a beautiful tapestry
with every situation you
experience.

Through His power,
even the most unlikely
circumstances can be
transformed.

He has seen all of your tears,
all of your pain,

and He longs to restore your joy.

He wants to resurrect all of your hopes and dreams.

A new day is about to dawn because

no mountain you face is greater
than His ability to help you.

Good things will
come your way again:

a smile after the tears;

a rainbow after the storm;

and a beautiful sunrise
after a long, dark night.

In the meantime,
take good care of yourself:

Spend a day in a hammock,

drink in the beauty
of God's creation,

meditate on your favorite psalm,

put on a pair of warm fuzzy slippers,

sniff a bouquet of beautiful flowers,

sit in front of a roaring fire,

treat yourself to your favorite dessert,

or curl up with a cup of tea and a
much-loved book.

Do whatever you need to do
to cherish who you are.

Surround yourself with
those special people you love

will be mine as well.

Kisses of
Encouragement

Kisses from a
Friend's Heart

Kisses of Love

Kisses from a
Mother's Heart

Kisses from a
Sister's Heart

HOWARD BOOKS
A DIVISION OF SIMON & SCHUSTER

New York   London   Toronto   Sydney